KT-555-843

KINGFISHER
An imprint of Kingfisher Publications Plc
New Penderel House
283-288 High Holborn
London WC1V 7HZ
www.kingfisherpub.com

First published by Kingfisher 2005
2 4 6 8 10 9 7 5 3 1

A CIP catalogue record for this book is
available from the British Library.

ISBN-13: 978 0 7534 1132 2

Printed in India
TS/0707/THOM/PICA(PICA)/90SES/F

HO HO HO!

150 CRACKING CHRISTMAS JOKES

KINGFISHER

**What Christmas carol
do parents like?**
Silent Night.

**Why does Santa
have three gardens?**
So he can hoe, hoe, hoe!

Knock Knock.
Who's there?
Hanna.
Hanna who?
**Hanna partridge
in a pear tree!**

Where do you find elves?
Depends where you left them!

What is green, covered with tinsel and says "Ribbet, ribbet"?
A mistle-toad.

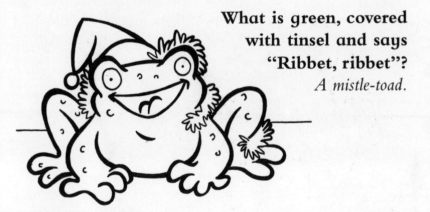

What's the best key to get at Christmas?
A turkey!

**What did
Mrs Claus say
to Santa Claus?**
*It looks like
rain, dear.*

**What squeaks
and is scary?**
*The Ghost of
Christmouse Past!*

**What does Frosty
the Snowman wear
on his head?**
An ice cap.

Who brings Christmas presents to police stations?
Santa Clues.

Why did the reindeer wear black boots?
Because his brown ones were all muddy.

What kind of bread do elves make sandwiches with?
Shortbread!

What happens when Frosty the Snowman gets dandruff?

He gets snowflakes.

Who brings Christmas presents to baby sharks?

Santa Jaws.

Who is never hungry at Christmas?

The turkey – he's always stuffed.

How many elves does it take to change a light bulb?

Ten. One to change the bulb and nine to stand on each other's shoulders.

How do chihuahuas say Merry Christmas?

Fleas Navidog!

Why didn't Santa Claus get wet when he lost his umbrella?

It wasn't raining.

Teacher: Can anyone name Santa's reindeer?

Anne: Dasher, Dancer, Prancer, Vixen, Comet, Cupid, Donner, Blitzen, Rudolph and Al.

Teacher: Are you sure about Al?

Anne: Yes – "Then Al the reindeer loved him…"

What does Frosty the Snowman's wife put on her face at night?
Cold cream.

Santa travels in a sleigh. What do elves travel in?
Minivans!

Waiter, Waiter, my turkey has gone off!
Which way did it go?

One Christmas, a teacher who hated giving homework, a nice babysitter and Santa Claus were riding in the lift of a very posh hotel. Just before the doors opened, they all noticed a ten-pound note lying on the floor. Which one picked it up?

Santa Claus, of course, because the other two don't exist!

Why are Christmas trees like bad knitters?
They both drop their needles!

What do reindeer always say before telling you a joke?
This one will sleigh you!

**Which of Santa's reindeers
needs to mind his manners
the most?**
Rude-olph.

**What is red and white and
goes up and down and
up and down?**
*Santa Claus stuck
in a lift.*

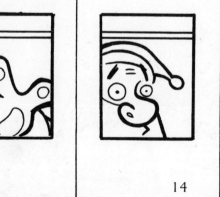

14

What goes "Ho ho ho, plop plop plop"? *Santa Claus in the toilet.*

This turkey tastes like an old sofa. *Well, you asked for something with plenty of stuffing.*

Who carries all of Santa's books? *His books elf.*

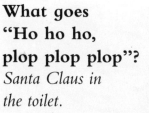

What does Frosty the Snowman eat for lunch?
Icebergers.

What's red and white and red and white and red and white?
Santa Claus rolling down a hill.

What do sheep say to each other at Christmastime?
Merry Christmas to ewe!

Why did the reindeer cross the road?
Because he was tied to a chicken.

Who lives at the North Pole, makes toys and rides around in a pumpkin?
Cinderelfa!

What goes "Ho, ho, swoosh! ho, ho, swoosh!"?
Santa caught in a revolving door.

Why does Santa Claus go down the chimney on Christmas Eve?
Because it soots him.

Where do Frosty the Snowman and his wife go to dance?
Snowballs.

How do you know if there's a reindeer in your refrigerator?
There are hoof prints in the butter.

Why did the elf sleep in the fireplace?
He wanted to sleep like a log.

How does Mickey Mouse get around during the winter?
Mice skates.

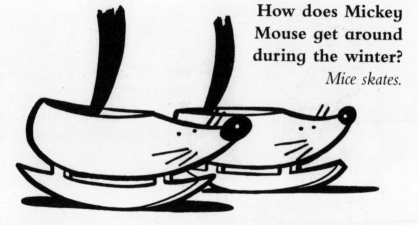

What can Santa give away and still keep?
A cold.

What did the dog breeder get when she crossed an Irish setter with a pointer at Christmastime?
A pointsetter.

What nationality are Santa and Mrs Claus?
North Polish.

Elf: Santa, one of the reindeer swallowed my pencil! What should I do?
Santa: Use a pen.

What do you call Frosty the Snowman on rollerblades?
A snowmobile.

How do you tell the difference between tinned turkey and tinned custard?
Read the labels.

How does Frosty the Snowman get around?
On an ice-icle.

My mum bought a huge turkey for Christmas dinner.
That must have cost a fortune.
Actually, she got it for a poultry amount.

What kind of bills do elves have to pay?
Jingle bills!

If Santa Claus and Mrs Claus had a child, what would he be called?
A subordinate clause.

What do you call a chicken at the North Pole?
Lost.

How long should an elf's legs be?
Just long enough to reach the ground!

Who is Frosty the Snowman's favourite aunt?
Aunt Arctica.

A boy went to the butcher's and saw that the turkeys were 90p a pound. He asked the butcher, "Do you raise them yourself?"
"Of course I do," the butcher replied. "They were only 50p a pound this morning!"

Joe: How come you never hear anything about the tenth reindeer, Olive?
Mary: Olive?
Joe: You know – Olive, the other reindeer, used to laugh and call him names...

24

If athletes get athlete's foot, what do elves get?
Mistle-toes.

What did the police officer say when he saw Frosty the Snowman stealing?
"Freeze!"

Who delivers presents to baby crabs?
Sandy Claws!

How does Rudolph know when Christmas is coming?
He looks at his calen-deer.

What kind of cake does Frosty the Snowman like?
Any kind, as long as it has lots of icing.

Where does Santa stay when he's on holiday?
At a ho-ho-hotel!

**What does Mrs Claus sing
to Santa on his birthday?**
*"Freeze a jolly
good fellow!"*

**What makes the turkey
such a fashionable bird?**
*He's always well dressed
when he comes to dinner!*

Knock knock.
Who's there?
Elf.
Elf who?
**Elf me wrap
this present
for Santa!**

Knock knock.
Who's there?
Holly.
Holly who?
**Holly up and elf
me wrap this
present for Santa!**

Knock knock.
Who's there?
Yule.
Yule who?
**Yule be sorry if
you don't holly
up and elf me
wrap this present
for Santa!**

Knock knock.
Who's there?
Snow.
Snow who?
**Snow time to be playing
games! Yule be sorry if you
don't holly up and elf me
wrap this present for Santa!**

Mum, can I have a dog for Christmas?
No, you can have turkey
like everyone else.

**Why does St Nicholas
have a white beard?**
*So he can hide at
the North Pole!*

**Why did they let
the turkey join
the band?**
*Because it had
the drumsticks.*

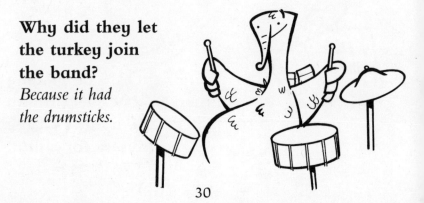

**What do you get if you
cross a snowman with
a vampire?**
Frostbite.

**What did the
sheep say to
the shepherd?**
Season's Bleatings!

**What do they call a
wild elf in Texas?**
Gnome on the range!

What do you call someone who doesn't believe in Father Christmas?
A rebel without a Claus.

What bird has wings but cannot fly?
Roast turkey.

What do you get when you cross Frosty the Snowman with a baker?
Frosty the Dough-man!

**What smells most
in a chimney?**
Santa's nose!

**What do reindeer
have that no
other animals on
earth have?**
Baby reindeer.

**What kind of pine
has the sharpest
needles?**
A porcupine.

**How do elves
greet one
another?**
*"Small world,
isn't it?"*

**What does Santa like
to have for breakfast?**
Mistle-toast.

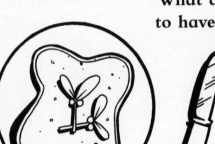

**Why does Santa take
presents to children
around the world?**
*Because the presents
won't take themselves!*

**What do you get if
you cross a bell
with a skunk?**
Jingle smells!

**What does Frosty the
Snowman drink?**
Iced tea.

**What's red and
green and guides
Santa's sleigh?**
*Rudolph the
red-nosed pickle.*

Why did the giraffe get a Christmas present?
To thank him for sticking his neck out for everyone.

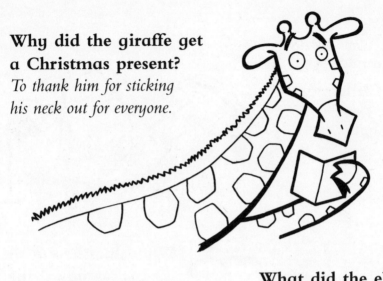

What did the elf say when he was teaching Santa Claus to use the computer?
"First, yule log in!"

What did the snowman's wife give him when she was angry with him?
The cold shoulder.

How do cows greet each other at Christmas?
Mooooory Christmas.

What does Santa use when he goes fishing?
His north pole!

How do you get into Donner's house?
You ring the deerbell!

What do vampires put on their turkey at Christmas?
Grave-y.

What is twenty feet tall, has sharp teeth and goes "Ho, ho, ho!"
Tyranno-santa Rex!

What kind of music do elves like best?
"Wrap" music.

How many reindeer does it take to change a light bulb?
Eight. One to screw in the bulb and the other seven to hold Rudolph down.

What's red and green and flies?
An airsick Santa!

What do you call an elf who steals gift wrap from the rich and gives it to the poor?
Ribbon Hood.

How did Rudolph learn to read?
He was elf-taught.

Where does Frosty the Snowman keep his money?
In a snow bank.

Why was Santa's little helper depressed?
He had low elf-esteem.

Where does Father Christmas go to vote?
The North Poll.

Why do elves scratch themselves?
Because they're the only ones who know where they're itchy!

What kind of motorcycle does Santa Claus ride?
A Holly Davidson.

What do you call Saint Nick after he has come down the chimney?
Cinder Claus!

Why does Santa Claus owe everything to the elves?
Because he is an elf-made man!

What does Frosty the Snowman call ice?
Skid stuff.

What's red and white and gives presents to gazelles?
Santelope.

What does Frosty the Snowman like to put on his icebergers?
Chilly sauce.

What goes "oh, oh, oh?"
Santa Claus walking backwards!

Who sings "Love me Tender" and makes Christmas toys?
Santa's Elvis.

What does Santa get if he's stuck in a chimney?
Claustrophobic!

What does Frosty the Snowman take when he gets sick?
A chill pill.

What did the bald man say when he got a comb for Christmas?
Thanks, I'll never part with it!

What do you call an elf who tells silly jokes?
A Christmas card!

Who delivers Christmas presents to dogs?
Santa Paws!

If I'm standing at the North Pole, facing the South Pole, and the east is on my left hand, what's on my right hand?
Fingers!

What did Adam tell his girlfriend on December 24th?
It's Christmas, Eve.

What's the difference between the Christmas alphabet and the ordinary alphabet?
No L (Noel).

What does Tarzan sing at Christmastime?
Jungle Bells.

How do you make an idiot laugh on New Year's Eve?
Tell him a joke on Christmas Day.

What is Santa's favourite breakfast cereal?
Frosted Flakes.

Did you know that all the angels in the heavenly choir had the same name?

Sure, haven't you ever heard the song, "Hark, the Harold Angels Sing"?

What did the Japanese tourist wear at the North Pole?

An Eskimono.

Mother: I know you're disappointed with your present, Billy, but remember, it's the thought that counts.

Billy: Couldn't you have thought a little bigger?

Where did the mistletoe go to become rich and famous?
Hollywood.

What do elves learn in school?
The Elf-abet.

David: Have you bought your grandmother's Christmas present yet, Susie?

Susie: No. I was going to get her a handkerchief, but I changed my mind.

David: Why?

Susie: I can't work out what size her nose is.

What's the best thing to put into your Christmas dinner?
Your teeth!

Why did the gingerbread man go to the doctor?
Because he was feeling crummy!

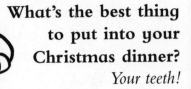

Where is the best place to put your Christmas tree?
Between your Christmas two and your Christmas four!

Knock knock.
Who's there?
Mary.
Mary who?
Merry Christmas!

Why do people cry at Christmastime?
Because they get santa-mental.

What do you get if you cross an apple with a Christmas tree?
A pineapple!

What do you have in December that you don't have in any other month?
The letter "D".

Doctor, doctor, help! I've swallowed some Christmas decorations.
Yes, I can see you have a touch of tinselitis.

Knock Knock.
Who's there?
Doughnut.
Doughnut who?
Doughnut open until Christmas!

Why is it so cold at Christmas?
Because it's in Decembrrrrr!

Why do mummies like Christmas so much?
Because of all the wrapping!

Knock Knock.
Who's there?
Holly.
Holly who?
Holly-days are here again!

**What kind of money
do they use at the
North Pole?**
Cold cash.

**Why should
Christmas dinner
always be
well done?**
*So you can say
"Merry Crispness!"*

Knock Knock.
Who's there?
Wayne.
Wayne who?
**Wayne in
a manger.**

What did one angle say to the other angel?
Halo there!

What falls down all the time at the North Pole, but never hurts itself?
Snow!

What's red, white and blue at Christmastime?
A sad candy cane.

There once was a Viking named Rudolph the Red. He was at home one day with his wife. He looked out the window and said, "Look, darling. It's raining."

She shook her head. "I don't think so, dear. I think it's snowing."

But Rudolph knew better, so he said, "Let's go outside and we'll find out."

They went outside and discovered that it was in fact raining. And Rudolph turned to his wife and said, "I knew it was raining. Rudolph the Red knows rain, dear!"

What Christmas carol is popular in the desert?
O camel ye faithful.

Knock, knock.
Who's there?
Wenceslas.
Wenceslas who?
Wenceslas bus home on Christmas Eve?

Why is it difficult to keep a secret at the North Pole?
Because your teeth chatter.

**What does a short-sighted
Christmas gingerbread
man use for eyes?**
Contact raisins.

**What do you call a
letter sent up the
chimney on
Christmas Eve?**
Black mail!

**What do angry
mice send each
other in
December?**
Cross mouse cards.

"Thanks for the electric guitar you gave me for Christmas," Timmy said to his uncle. "It's the best present I ever got."

"That's great," said his uncle. "Do you know how to play it?"

"Oh, I don't play it. My mum gives me a pound a day not to play it during the day, and my dad gives me five pounds a week not to play it at night!"

Why did Frosty the Snowman go to live in the middle of the ocean?
Because snowman is an island...

How do sheep in Mexico say Merry Christmas?
Fleece Navidad!

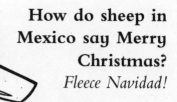

Who works in a department store selling perfume at Christmas?
Frank Incense.

What was so good about the neurotic doll Jenny got for Christmas?
It was wound up already.

What do you get if you deep-fry Santa Claus?
Crisp Cringle.

What do reindeer hang on their Christmas trees?
Hornaments.

What sort of ball doesn't bounce?
A snowball.

What do you call a bunch of chess grandmasters bragging about their games in a hotel lobby?
Chess nuts boasting in an open foyer!

What's the best thing to give your parents at Christmas?
A list of everything you want.

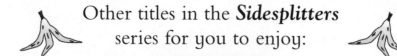

Other titles in the *Sidesplitters* series for you to enjoy: